My Four Lives

Dr. Alberto Giuseppe Valmori

To order additional copies of this book, contact:
Xlibris
844-714-8691
www.Xlibris.com
Orders@Xlibris.com

ISBN: Softcover   978-1-6641-2201-7
       EBook   978-1-6641-2208-6

Print information available on the last page

Rev. date: 08/21/2020

My Four Lives

Since 16/03/2020 I have been inside my flat due to the Coronavirus regulations here in Malta.

After two weeks I have decided to go back to my life events and write them down, first to pass the time and second just in case I will start forgetting all that has gone on.

I was born in Florence (Italy) on the 13th of September 1935 in a flat that did not have much light as my Parents were starting their life together on a small budget.

My Mother always told me that I was born at Midday, the wrong way round and my Father was going crazy seeing that I was a boy and he was afraid that I will not live.

I always thought that it was very advanced of my Father to be witnessing my birth considering that it was 1935 and men were not supposed to witness the birth of their children.

Eighteen months later my Sister was born and to this date we are very close, I speak to her every week

From Malta, she lives in London.

We moved to a Flat, in the Centre of Florence, on the top floor near the San Lorenzo Cathedral, that had a lot of light but was very hot in the summer and very cold in the winter, but we were a very Happy Family.

A problem that I remember well was that my Father suffered from T.B. (Tuberculosis). In those days there were not Antibiotics, hence there was not a proper cure.

Sometimes my Father used to take us children out for a walk, but occasionally we had to come back quickly as he was not feeling well.

Especially in the winter our flat was cold for him and we had lots of steep stairs, so he used to stay at my Grandfather Emilio's place, which was centrally heated and had a lift, it was in Via Calimala 2 in the best part of Florence.

It was also my Grandfather Emilio Accountancy Office. He was a well known and respected Public Accountant in Florence.

My Sister and I went to the kindergarten run by the Nuns, I remember coming back home with girls pants as I had soiled mine! To this day I remember the funny feeling.

My Primary school was just round the corner and was called Davanzati.

My first teacher's name was Miss Schiatti, I remember her with affection, she was very dedicated and fair.

We used to hang around outside the school as our Parents did not worry, they knew that we were enjoying our friends.

Now I remember that I like to box with my friends, as some of the Parents complained to me.

Later when I was 14 years old I went for boxing at the SEMPRE AVANTI JUVENTUS Gym.

The middle school was also close by the San Lorenzo Cathedral.

The first year was a bit of a shock, it was serious study, Latin Algebra, Italian Literature and Poetry, were hard at first, but then it was O.K

My Grandfather Emilio did a research into our Ancestors and found out that our Family name Valmori were known in Florence since the year 1212! They were famous Surgeons, Judges and some of them were buried in the Church of Santo Spirito, a burial reserved for important citizens. They use to marry with another Family called Fantoni and often the two Families Shields were shown together ; but I never met a Fantoni of my age! Anyway Families no longer are making alliances through marriages!

The Second World War started and my Family decided to evacuate to the Countryside for safety.

We went to Greve in Chianti to stay with my Father's Wet Nurse, a very nice lady, that had always kept in touch with us. We had just one room and one bed and the four of us slept in it.

My Father unfortunately broke a leg and was in plaster, so it was difficult for the four of us to sleep in one bed.

So my Sister went to stay with the Family Medical Doctor, near by, they did not have any children so she was very loved and spoiled with good food and attention.

I was sent far out of the village to a Farming Family that I think was very happy to have me as cheap labour.

I was, in fact, assigned 33 sheeps, no dog, to take them out and find grazing all day and bring them back at night.

I was very stressed at first, because I never been away from my Family and everything was new to me.I remember for cleaning the chickens coop I used to be given, as reward, a fresh egg!

I soon became good as a shepherd, moving the flock to good grazing and not loosing any sheep.I was barking like a dog and throwing stones to make the sheeps move.I met other shepherds we use to wrestle and then I discovered that I had a natural ability for this sport

After about eight months, thinking that life in Florence had gone back to normal, we decided to go back to Florence.

My friends were laughing at me because I was speaking like a Country boy, but they were very happy to have me back. The air raids continued and sometimes we had to run to the shelter four or five times a day.The air shelter was deep down in the San Lorenzo Cathedral, and we used to scare each other by playing Ghosts ! We borrow some white sheets and look and sound like real Ghosts.

To this day when I hear the sound of Spitfire Planes I feel like running away!

Later we became trapped in our flat. We had the Italian Snipers on the roofs shooting at the German Soldiers and the Allies Army were advancing in the City and we could not move.

I remember we had a storm and my Father was collecting water from the leaking roof gutters. My Father put some grains on the kitchen marble top to attract pigeons and then close the window and trap them . I remember they were a bit hard but very welcome as we had no meat. We had a lot of aubagines and for many years I could not eat them!

My Sister and I with two large flask of Chianti we used to go and collect water from an emergency fountain on the road. We had to make several trips and go up sixty steep stairs to our flat. The lack of water was really hard to take and we were really happy to help with this job .Eventually life went back to normal and we went back to school on a regular basis.

The middle school was a mixed school so this was new to study with girls and competing for their attention. Because of this, one of my best friends, challenged me to a serious boxing match, I tried to refuse because I really liked my friend but he was adamant, and all other boys were pushing us to do it. We went to a place called Fortezza da Basso an old Army Fort with gardens and quiet places by the big walls and started to fight. I really wanted to finish quickly as I did not like to hurt my friend, but having a natural ability I broke his nose.

The word went round the school and I had to fight the biggest boys of the school, luckily for me I was faster than them.

Since I was nine years old my Father used to bring home work that needed checking and adding figures up, no calculators, so I was very happy to help him and he trusted me with the quality of my work.

My Grandfather Emilio and my Father were Accountants and although I could do this type of work I wanted to be in the open air and not in a office.

On the 1st August 1949 my Father died. That day we were supposed to go on holydays to the seaside so it was even a bigger shock .It has been for me a long life pain and I missed him so much and I was very unhappy.

I decided to follow my instinct and by September 1949 I joined the Agricultural College Called CASCINE on the outskirts of Florence. I cycled, in all weathers, to the College, which was a big change as previously all schools were near by.

Even here same story, the biggest boy in my class tried to beat me up, but I knocked him down and we were lucky not to be suspended. He tried again and I knocked him down, the word got round and the, the ones of other classes wanted to fight . I said this time I do not want to be expelled, if you want to fight me come to the boxing club SEMPRE AVANTI JUVENTUS and we box in the ring. However after me you will have to box with the best boxing champions of Florence. Because of this nobody accepted the challenge and the matter was closed.

One day the Teacher of Physical education brought to school some boxing gloves, and when my turn came I gave him a good one. He stopped and told me that he did not know that I was a trained boxer, I should have warned him! I also played for the College Volley Ball in the First Team and we used to play against other schools. I was also good at Pole Vaulting .

One of my best friends as school James Petrucci suggested that we get a tent and do a tour of Italy by cycle during our holydays. His Mother was American and she convinced my Mother to let us go on the tour .It was a wonderful experience, we went from Florence to the Italian Alps and found snow and then down to the hot South and back to Florence. We lost a lot of weight but we made it!

At this point my Father's Brother Giuseppe saw that my Mother was needing financial help and some assistance with us the two children, he had not children himself, so started to care for us.

He was then a very rich man, but having started from nothing he did not want to spoil us.

In my spare time and on part of my holydays I used to go to his Tyres Factory and be a factory worker, he was more strict with me than with his workers!

On the plus side, I was "Bedding the Tyres" in for the Clients.This gave me the opportunity to drive many makes of cars:Fiat, Lancia, Maserati, Ferrari, Porches etc.

I will never thank my Uncle enough for getting me used to hard work, as later in life I have been able to get over any problems that I encountered. On the plus side my Uncle had a Villa in Lido di Camaiore, a seaside resort, on the Tirreno Sea about 90 KM from Florence .I used to cycle there so I had my bicycle for the holyday. My Cousin Johnny was also there, he lived and is still living in Milan and to this day we are like Brothers as we spent so many summers together.

When I completed the five years of Agricultural College I got a job as Assistant Farm Manager. I was very happy with the job, it was what I always wanted to do ; and I was doing it well, the problem was the life style. I was really a City boy, used to sport and social life, all this was missing. I gave it nearly a year, just not to give up easily, the Manager was happy with my work but he, being a Country boy, understood that City life was too different, and that I missed it.

Thanks to my Uncle Giuseppe I was able to enrol at Economics and Commerce University of Florence that was then located at Villa Favard a walking distance from my home.

By this time my Sister Luisa was completing her Classic Piano Graduation from the Conservatorio Cherubini in Florence, She did well and was also playing on the Italian Radio.

I had not mentioned that at the age of 16 I became very short sighted so I changed from Boxing to Greek Roman Wrestling and I was able to go back to this sport whilst at University. At the University there is the tradition that the first year students buy the Seniors a lot of cigarettes, I was a bit naughty because I did not want to follow the tradition. So when the Seniors wanted to force me to pay I through a couple of people against the wall and told them that my wrestling friends are dying to come and put you in hospital. I have always felt bad about doing this. I study and continue to help my Uncle Giuseppe at the Factory, whenever I could. He bought me a VESPA 150 cc and this was a great help to carry Girls as by this time Italy had become prosperous and you needed at least a VESPA!

My life at University went well, I continued Greek Roman Wrestilng, did some work for my Uncle Giuseppe, had a very nice girlfriend who was studying Mathematics at the University of Florence. I had passed all exams but the remaining one was English. The Lady Professor of English was very competent but expected a good standard. I did not want to get just a pass so I decided to go to London. Of course it was the swinging sixties and I liked the experience.

I then decided to write my Thesis on British materials . This would have obliged me to improve my English and probably my Professors would have found it interesting.

So at the beginning of 1959 I started writing my Thesis on "THE ECONOMICAL EFFECTS OF THE BRITISH PURCHASE TAX".

At this time I started to study all this type of Taxes in Other European Countries and also in U.S.A. With these studies I proved that the BRITISH PURCHASE TAX was not a very good Tax.

In my Thesis I stated that "THE BRITISH PURCHASE TAX" should be replaced by the French TVA, at that time only France was using this Tax.

Exactly 13 Years later the British Government introduced the VAT which was exactly the TVA, confirming my Thesis.

To pay for my living in London I was selling shoes in Dolcis Shoe Shop in Oxford Street. A friend of mine came to London with a range of shoes samples from Factories in Tuscany but could not get any orders. I asked him to leave the samples with me and that I will try to sell. With beginner's luck I landed an order from British Shoe Corporation for 10,000 pairs one model one colour! This was a very large order and when I went to Italy I met a very experienced and successful Representative of many Italian Shoes Manufactures and I teamed up with him. He had a very big American Car Pontiac Catalina, pink with white top and we used to go to Germany and other European Countries to show the samples in First Class Hotels, having with us beautiful girls to model the shoes, to take orders from the local shops.

I got my Doctorate Degree in Economics and Commerce in July 1961 and on 13th December 1961 I married my First British Wife, it was a good marriage and it lasted until 1983. With my Wife and Daughter I was in Florence buying shoes for a British Company.

After a couple of years my Wife wanted to look after her aging Parents, very lovely people, so they started living with us in London. My Wife's Father died whilst living with us. Her Mother lived with us until she also passed away, having looked after my Daughter very well. I was working very hard and so was my Wife, hence you can say that my Mother in Law brought my Daughter up. I just remember the first time she met me she was very suspicious, thinking I was marrying her Daughter to get the British Passport !

After she became like my Mother and I could not do anything wrong! I have many fond memories of her, of course she was with us many years!

My Uncle Giuseppe was really a very rich man and my friends were always telling me that I did not need to work, luckily enough I never listened to them. When my Auntie died my Uncle lost his way and all his fortune. I had acquired an agricultural property in San Giovanni Valdarno that consisted of a vineyard and an establishment for horses. My Uncle had originally made his first money with horses with his ability to buy and sell horses. So I offered him the use of this property and he was quickly able to go back to his old skills and make money with horses.

I was on holiday with my Family and we went to visit him. He had a very nice horse and he asked me if I wanted to ride it. To this day I cannot forget the look of happiness in his face to see that I was a good rider.

Sadly one early morning my Uncle was cycling back home, having fed the horses, when he was knocked down by a car. He fell on his head and died almost instantly .Of course I came from London for his funeral and I felt obliged to carry his coffin remembering how much he had done for me and my Sister.

Perhaps I did not mention before but when I left Florence to go back to London I stopped buying or selling shoes and went back to my old skills as Accountant .I worked for several Companies and at the beginning of 1976 I agreed with my Wife that I shall go for two years, to work in the Middle East as I wanted a change of scenery .

Before going I had already paid my house in London and paid most of the Villa in Spain. It was more for adventure than for financial need that I took this job in Oman. I was interviewed in London in English but of course, when I got there everything was in Arabic. The hotel where I was the Accountant belonging to the Sultan of Oman BIN QBUS, and his Son took over, as a young progressive man, he only recently died.

I reorganized the Hotel accounting and costing systems, later opened a large supermarket and all this was very appreciated. I remember the first time I went alone to the local market, therewere all these people with shining daggers and I was the only European there. Everybody was looking at me, but I felt that they only wanted to be friendly

One year in Oman went very well, and then this happened . In the evening, at the bar, we Europeans could drink alcohol, and of course, I was there with the other Guests. One evening they asked me if we could go to have a drink in another place, just to get out of the hotel, I agreed and took them in the car assigned to me.

Coming out of the bar we met a road block, I got into an argument with the Policeman so I was asked to go to the Hospital. Thinking nothing of it I met the English Nurse and she asked me if I had any drinks, I said, just a very small beer, as I was driving. She said I am sorry for you but you are in trouble because this test reacts on a trace of alcohol . In fact the blood test came positive. I was taken to the local prison and when I entered in this room there were about 50 people and I was the only European. I decided to stay calm and lay on the concrete floor and pretended, at first, to sleep, later because of tiredness and the intensive heat, I really fell asleep. In the morning the food came in a flat large container and everybody put t heir hands in it and started eating, I did the same to show that I am like them. At this point they all became friendly and asked me to stay by the door were the air conditioning was coming from the offices, so I would be more comfortable.

I was there 48 hours and found out that the people were there for small offences. Eventually I was free but a few days later I had to go to the Tribunal and receive the sentence, a fine that was paid by the Sultan. In this job I could go to London every six months for two weeks.

It was near the time to go for my holyday when I met, at the hotel 's bar, people that were scouts for the Italian Government (Construction). We got to know each other and they told me that the Italian Government was building in Bandar Abbas (Iran) the third largest port in the World employing 10,000 people of 27 different Nationalities, but they had a problem. I asked what sort of problem? The Administration and Finance Director worked from the Capital Teheran more than 1,000 KM from the construction site and did not want to live and work at 51 Centigrade on a building site of 20 square KM in a semi deserted place. In those days there was no internet,good telephone, scan machines etc. So the Admin and Personnel problems were falling on the Technical Head of the project creating many complications and inefficiencies. They said that having seen how I work and having made a few enquiries, considering how I managed, I could be a possible choice, providing I was going to stay on the Construction site. I said I am already at 51 Centigrade I should find it possible to work there. They asked me if on my way to London I could meet the Head of Personnel responsible for this project in Rome. I had planned to stop in Rome to meet my Uncle Gianni, so I agreed to go for the interview .

I was offered the job, in those days not many Italians have a good knowledge of English, and Italy was booming so qualified people prefer to stay in Italy. After my holiday I must go directly to Iran as the need is URGENT.

So I did not go back to Oman and I never went back there again, I think because the Sultan was very annoyed.

The job in Iran was challenging but had a lot of advantages.

I had a beautiful 5 bedrooms bungalow and my Family could join me, but the two of them came only once. On our residential part of the Project we had Church, Mosque, Hospital, Swimming Pools,Tennis Courts,Squash Courts, Table Tennis and Horses for riding on the beach. In England I did a lot of horse riding, so in my free time, I rode a lot.

To keep the staff amused we organized a lot of Tennis, Squash, Table Tennis tournaments and the standards were surprising high and we all improved and enjoyed.

Then in 1979 the Iranian Revolution happened .My Wife was with me at the time and she was lucky to go out on the flight organized by the Italian Government.

The works had to stop, but in case of Revolution, we had a price revision formula that eventually made a lot of money to the Project.

A lot of our workers were from Asian Countries and were sent back with buses.

The problem remain for the Italian workers that could not be evacuated by bus. I went to Dubai and chartered a fast boat . At the time Dubai had only one good Hotel, the Sheraton on the Creek. When I went back to Dubai, many years later, I could not believe how it had changed. The boat that I chartered was used to supply the Oil Rig Platforms. It had to be fast to overrun the Iranian corvettes because by then they were blocking the Straight of Hormuz. The American Captain of our boat had been in the Vietnam War and he was up to the challenge. We could only transport 60 passengers at the time so I did many trips with them, as if I was on the boat they felt more safe. In this sort of work you have a lot of power but you also need to be trusted and luckily I was.

The Iranian Revolutionary invaded our site but all machinery and vehicles had been welded together so they went empty handed. They destroyed our wines and Spirits, which I understand, but the table tennis rackets no!!

The next problem caused by being closed inside the camp was that we extracted the water for drinking and the works from the sea by way of a desalination plant. Of course the fuel started t getting low and in the desert we would have died. The Project Manager called me and confessed that he was afraid to go out of the camp because he had a lot of enemies but he said that I had a good reputation as a just man and that I should go to the Town 50 KM away. Then go to the Bank and pay for 15 Diesel Tankers, then drive back at the head of the caravan. He suggested that I could go out with a different car and disguised, if I felt more comfortable . I obviously agree to do this job as the alternative was too horrible to contemplate. However I decided to use my car a Fiat 132 that the mechanics for fun had turned it into a very fast car .So I knew that, if I could pass the first obstacle, the Revolutionaries with their Hillman Minx could not catch me. So it was, the gates open and I rushed out,they follow after me, but their cars were no match for my Fiat 132. I arrived at the Bank, got the cash out, and organized the caravan. The Town was happy to see some activities, because 700 of our own Iranian workers had lost their job. So I made my way back at the head of the caravan of 15 Diesel tankers, carrying the precious Diesel.

Life continued inside the camp and to try and keep peace we did hire a few Iranians, in the hope that the Revolution will calm down. The Financial Controller of one of our Subcontractors, we had 16, went to the Town but on the way back, he was kidnapped, and he quickly organized the payment for his dismissed Iranian workers. Of course the same happened to me, but I was with our Interpreter, so I was able to explain to them that it was not my money and I will never pay, you are better off to let me go and I will see if I can get you more work. Our Interpreter was very respected and he told them that, I am a good man,but that I stick to my words, they are better off to let me go, which they did.

Of course this went round the camp and then to Rome H.O and together with what I had done before everybody was very impressed.

Even my Uncle Gianni in Rome heard about this and he told me when I saw him next.

After the Revolution the war with Iraq started and our Port was the only supply route that Iran could access, and it helped to Iran to win the war.

My Wife was very afraid for me and she begged me to come out of Iran. I agreed and at the end of 1980 I resigned and came home .

I was offered by one of the Companies of the Group a six months mission to Saudi Arabia. The project consisted of the Construction, for the Saudi Government, of the University of Taif. The project organisation was based in Geddah on the Red Sea.

I arrived there in the night, very tired, and I did not see that our Guest House was next to the Mosque. At four A.M the Muezzin started his prayer and I shoot out of the bed thinking somebody was in the room! Not a problem the following day as I had got used to it.

After a few days I went,with the driver and jeep, through the desert to Taif, this is a quiet place high up and much cooler than the desert. I remember every day, about 5 b P.M, a strong wind would come, and everything that was not really heavy would fly up, and then come down again. I started to work on site with just one staff to do the salaries . I told H.O how many people I needed to run this site and they promised me that they were recruiting. In the meantime, I had to do all the work without staff and air conditioning. I told H.O I will manage for six months, according to contract, but if staff is not recruited I cannot continue. They saw that the work was getting done so no staff came. At the end of the six months I did not extend the contract and went back home. The staff that came after me were twelve people, no wonder I was killing myself with work!

The Fiat Group (Construction) got the Contract to build the Naval Base in Homs (Lybia). This was a much smaller project that employed 1,700 people, after Iran it felt small for me. Originally this Project was started by a Turkish Company that built well the Offices and Accommodation but did not have the Technology and the know how to build the port, breakwaters etc. The very experienced FIA(IMPREGILO) had the equipment and know how and so I was given a good Family accommodation, car and driver. I had what would have been the Admiral office, the biggest and best office of my life! I often had to go to Tripoli to meet the people in the Ministry and, of course, make sure that the U.S.A Dollars payments were on time. The money went directly to Milan H.O, but because the U.S.A Dollar was getting very strong, H.O was not sending me back the money for local wages and expenses. We Italians were paid directly from H.O. But the local workers had to be paid in local currency with the funds from the Construction Site. I had to keep workers from Asia and a few Lybians calm as they wanted to go on strike.

As the Contract was in English, all correspondence had to be in English, I was able, without using bad words, to insult H.O for creating problems for me.

The works progressed very well and by the end of 1981 it was boring for me. The opening of a construction site is exciting but the closing is not. My holidays were due on my way to London I stopped in Milan and was introduced to the Directors of a Company employing 5,000 Nigerians Constructing Roads. I thought this was interesting but my Wife was not happy to come to Nigeria as she had a bad feeling about it.

I negotiated a good salary and I told her that I could not really refused. The Nigerian based Company was called Italcontractors and was building 10 roads all over Nigeria. Nigeria is a much bigger Country then how it appears on the maps. To go from one construction site to the other I had to use the plane. This surprised me but I found out that only the airlines pilots use maps that reflect the true size. Apparently due to Colonial Wars of the past, the maps are not drawn to the real size.

I was based at H.O in Lagos the then Capital of Nigeria and lived in a very nice villa in Apapa one of the best residential areas. In Lagos, because of heavy traffic, cars with even plates are used one day and the following day cars with odd plates are allowed to travel. So I had a Mercedes and a Volvo and of course a driver.

The work was not difficult as the staff were well trained and smart. It was mainly a question of being well accepted by the Governors of the various States as it was not always easy to meet their needs.

My personal life this time was different, before I was on building sites in Muslim Countries, without social life outside our building sites.

Lagos is now a City of 25 Million people with a lot of temptations. As my Wife was not coming to Lagos I started a relationship with a local woman who became my Second Wife. When this became serious the first problem I had was to move from the very nice villa to an apartment, still in Apapa, because the Managing Director did not want to live next door to a black woman.

My recent Wife had four children, she started very early in life like a lot of Nigerian Women .Two of the four boys the first and second born came to live with us, the others remained with their Fathers. I managed to place them in the best school in Lagos, them being intelligent boys, were doing well and were well behaved. When the time for our holidays came, the four of us went to Rome and Florence where they met my Family. The next holyday we went to my Villa in Spain and we enjoyed.

Later the first born decided to go back to his Father as probably his Father was putting pressure on him.

For the second born we decided, because he clearly wanted to stay with us, to send him to a very good private College in England near Leicester. He did very well, went to Lincoln College Oxford and won many scholarships . When he finished his Phd in Genetics he went for two year to Tokio on a sponsorship research assignment. During his holidays he always got a job and was always very independent.

Going back to my life in Lagos, times were changing and what the Directors had done to us, to make us move out of the villa into the flat made me very popular with all the staff making my job even easier. When trouble came I was always sheltered from it because they knew that I was not a racist.

The Italian Directors probably would have asked me to go, but they were afraid of the reaction of the Nigerian Directors that had 55% of the shares of the Company.

On the 8th of January 1984 my second Daughter was born in Lagos and, of course, she was the first mixed race child to be born in Italcontractors. The hospital where she was born was very good, and because on average in Nigeria a woman has five children they are very experienced. The work and Family life continued peacefully but when there was a regime change from Military to Civil, armed robberies became more frequent. One evening my telephone was not working and I decided to drive to our Guest House, still in Apapa, to make the calls. I was waiting for the gate to open, when a car came behind me and four armed robbers came out and pointed their guns at me. They came inside my car and took my ring and wallet. Not satisfied with that, they told me to drive to my flat as they were sure I must have more money there. I started driving around not wanting to go to my flat, one of the men was pressing his gun into my neck very hard, in fact the bruise remained a long time. On the way they stopped at another place, and shot one of the guards there. This attracted some Germans Expatriates that were armed, then the four armed men decided to go away, but the one that had been pressing his gun in my neck, I think decided to shoot me in the legs, but his gun jammed and I was safe. I went to thank the Germans for saving me and then drove home.

I was involved again in another armed robbery attempt, in the evening I was driving my Wife to visit some friends, when she spotted a car behind, she told me we have armed robbers behind, so I drove very fast back to our home, our gate opened in time and we were safe.

We were having a party at our Guest House when one of our cars, in which inside one of our Managers and his Wife entered the compound, but inside there were also two armed robbers. When they came out of the car one of the Directors was very quick to get a rifle used for elephant hunting, and started shooting. The armed robbers run away because they did not know how well armed we were.

So in the night we could no longer go out . When the Army Regime came back and started public firing executions of armed robbers, things went back quiet again and life went back to normal.

I was having problems with the Expatriate Directors as they did not like that the staff were with me and they thought that I was trying to be on the side of the Nigerian Directors ; I was just doing my job in the interest of the Company as fairly as possible.

I contacted the FIAT Group(Construction) to see if they had a suitable position. So in 1985 my Family and I went to Zaire now called the DCR (Democratic Republic of Congo) in Bukavu on the Eastern side of the Country.

The Company was building a Dam and a Power Station to supply electricity to Zaire Rwanda and Burundi and it was in a very strategic position. I often had to go to Bujumbura the Capital of Burundi to coordinate payments and other matters for the three Countries. I had to be careful not to travel at night as the drank soldiers at check points had the bad habit of firing!

I remember in Bujumbura, by the lake, there was a good French Restaurant and I could see the Hippopotamus and crocodiles in the lake.

I often thought that if I remained in Florence all my life if I would have been happy and safe or if I would have been bored without all this excitement.

On this project having a Nigerian Wife was making things easier for me, the Governor of Bukavu was inviting me and my Wife to their private functions and everything was fine.

Our camp consisted of very nice prefabricated housed on top of the hill and the construction site was at the bottom of the valley. The road down was a temporary one and during the tropical storms very slippery. It was very scary, like dying a few times a day, as you can imagine the the drop on the side was very deep.

At the camp there were tennis courts, so during my free time, I was playing . After a while I found out that there was, not far from the camp, a horse riding establishment, where people were doing horse jumping in the night, because during the day it was too hot . As horse riding was one of my favourite sports I bought a ¾ bread horse, very tall an ex racer, it was not an easy ride but I enjoyed, even if a few times I fell off and it was a long way down !

Because of work I had to go to the Capital of Zaire Kinshasa, of course by air, as it is a big Country.

My young Daughter was growing well but I was thinking that one day we would go back to Europe and she should start soon to see how life was in Europe. There I would not have two drivers and stewards and life would be normal.

I thought of asking in H.O FIAT Group(Construction) if I could send my Family to Florence (Tuscany) on my next holiday and go to another project on Bachelor Status as I thought the time had come for them to experience Europe. They told me that there was an opportunity in Niger, and because my French was good I could go.

The project was the construction of a road based in Zinder.

My colleague before me wanted to stay as much as possible in the Capital Niamey, on the River Niger, where we had an office. Now that the most important work was in Zinder I told them I would go to the Capital once a month as it was probably sufficient. The distance from Zinder to Niamey was exactly 1,000 KM, the road was very straight and good (we had constructed it).

My Driver was driving towards Niamey and the road was free but he stated to use the brakes, when some Antilopes crossed the road, we could have had a bad accident if the Driver had not started braking. After a few kilometres, same story, this time Camels came across the road. This happened a few times and when we got safely to Niamey I asked the Driver how does he do it? He told me he feels he has to slow down and he follows his instinct.

When I left this job as Administration and Finance Director I bought a very good radio for the Driver to thank him to have saved my life a few times.

After about a year the work on the site was finished and I went back to my Family in Italy. They had enjoyed their time there and made friends. They did not encounter racism and if occasionally somebody was curious the fact that the little girl was Italian cleared any suspicion.

I had left Italy a long time ago and realize that that I was too used to work abroad to try and work in Italy.

So we went back to Lagos (Nigeria) and found the same type of work I had before but with a different Company.

We lived in a beautiful villa in Ikeja, a very nice residential Area. I had four guards,, stewart, nanny,driver of course all paid by the Company. The work was quite easy and, when free, I played squash in air conditioned court.

All went well until June 1988. At this point my little girl felt ill, the local Doctor could not understand what it was ; but she was not getting any better. Luckily our Company Doctor, a Pakistani, came back from his holiday, he had been an Emathologist and he told us that all the symptons were LUKAEMIA and an URGENT blood test was organized to confirm and it was LUKAEMIA. The Doctor told me that if I want to save her life she needs an immediate large blood transfusion, luckily my blood type was suitable. After he told me that this sickness does not exist in Nigeria that is why the other Doctor could not recognise it. The only solution was to take her to Italy or London.

I checked with Italy but could not be sure that they would cure her, then I spoke to the Children Hospital in London and they told me that I was entitled to cure her as, luckily my Social Contributions were up to date . So end of July we travelled to London. The Mother was so distressed that she was making the little girl really afraid. When we got to the Hospital I realize that my Wife was not in condition to look after her and visit the hospital every day.

So I told the Company that I could not go back to Nigeria because my Wife was not in condition to look after my little girl by herself. After about a month I saw that my little girl was responding well to the Chemotherapy treatment, so naturally I had to start looking for a job.

The Finance Director and Company Secretary of Simms and Russel Ltd, a 150 Years Old Construction Company was retiring so I applied for this job.

I got the position on the understanding that for one year I would not make any changes. Once they knew that that I had to go to Hospital every day, they were very understanding, even the staff, I will never forget this. After one year I presented to the Board my proposals of reorganisation and they were accepted, I was with this Company from 1988 to 1995 when the Company was sold.

In these seven years many things went on in my life. My Wife encountered racism and this was very hard for us all. At the beginning we rented a house but my Wife was not happy there, I had bought her a new car for her to take the little girl to school, but she had some minor accidents and so she gave up driving. I had a Company car Ford Granada Automatic 2.9 cc and every two years we changed it for a new one.

Hoping to make my Wife happy I bought a four bedrooms house with Garage in Thamesmead, it was a bit of a drive for me but the little girl school was near by and there was no need to drive her to school. Again racial problems started with the neighbours making life difficult. Of course they were nice to me but when I was not there, problems.

To try and solve this problem I rented this house and moved outside London to Peterborough, a nice small City. The house was brand new with five bedrooms and double garages near a nature reserve with a big lake and lots of wild life.

It was a long drive for me so I started to remain in the Company flat, above the offices, from Monday to Friday. It was good for me but it made it more difficult for my Wife ; she started again having problems with the neighbours.

When my little girl was seven years old, I decided that for her to be with her Mother all the time was not good for her progress, so I placed her for one year at Grace Dieu Manor

House School and then for nine years to the Convent School "The Towers" Upper Beading West Sussex.

It was very hard for her to start with, but then sports and companionship with the other girls worked well. They were like Sisters, at time fighting, but having a healthy life. She became very good at Karate and other sports and she was very disciplined. To this day I do not know how I managed to pay the school fees when things started to go wrong.

My Wife mental health deteriorated and she attacked me and she bit me in my left leg. I had to go to hospital and I told them that a dog had bitten me . They did not believe me, they said these are human teeth marks, we have to tell the Police. I begged them not to as we have a young daughter and I do not want the Mother in prison.

A few days later the Social Services came to interview us. After several visits they convinced me that I was at risk and by then I was sixty years old, so they suggested a home for old people. There I would be safe and independent and I would have an apartment inside the structure with kitchen, bathroom, living room and one bedroom.

This was located in Colindale North London.

One day my Wife telephoned me that she could no longer live in Peterborough as she had too many problems. She said she will come, here where I am, pending the time I can find her another house in London. So she came with my young Daughter, who was on holiday at the time. I had of course to sleep on the floor!

At this point my Step Son came back from Japan and I rented a room for him in the same structure, so that we could all eat together.

The Manager of this establishment was a very good Lady and tried to resolve this difficult situation. The house in Peterborough was taken by the Bank because my Wife refused to let the Government pay for the mortgage, another sign of the mental problems she had at the time. She was given a flat in North London and at least I had my freedom back. By this time the Company was sold and I found myself, at sixty years old, without a job. Of course at sixty would have been very difficult to get a good job of the level I was used to.

So I thought that with all the experience that I have acquired, after working many years, I must find a way forward. At this time there were many Italian Companies and Wealthy individuals that wanted to start activities in London. I prepared a presentation and contacted the the Italian Chamber of Commerce in London, the Italian Trade Office, the Italian Institute for Culture and the Italian Church run by the Pallottini Fathers.

I found that my experience and qualifications were needed in the Market. At first I was meeting the Clients in their Hotels as I could not ask them to come to Old People's home ; other times I met them in Italian Restaurants in the centre of London.

I was successful to acquire Clients and able to pay my young Daughter's school fees, also thanks to the patience of the Convent Sisters. When she completed her studies at the Convent School at Upper Beading West Sussex I enrolled her in Oxford in the St.Clare's College a very prestigious College. Again it was a struggle to pay the fees, but later she got a scholarship for part of the fees, and things became easier for me.

I was, of course, seeing her whenever I could and she was doing well. I enroled her at the University of Birmingham Faculty of Social Sciences. Five years later she obtained her BS (HONS) Degree with her Dissertation Based on the People of African Origin.

In the Summer of that year she came to my office for a bit of work experience and she liked it.

From there on she was an amazing worker . I always had to tell her to go home as she had done so much work and still wanted to continue. She was happy and I was delighted for her and for me.

We decided to rent a very nice office in the City of London and everything was progressing well,all Clients were very happy with her work.

Her Mother sold the flat in North London. With the help of one of my Clients, and in the name of a Company, we bought a very nice house in Wembley where my Daughter and Wife went to live. I was still living in the same place in Colindale as I got used to be there.

In April 2008 the Law for Foreign Residents changed and I decided, also to give more responsibility to my Daughter, to move to Lille (France).

By Eurostar train I was able to get to the Centre of London in one hour, about the same time to come from a Suburb of London!

Everything was going well, my Daughter was running the office well and I was visiting Clients in Italy and other places. I was enjoying my life in Lille, playing table tennis with people of my age, and socialising . We used to go for table tennis competitions and then, sometimes, organize lunches and enjoy each other company. I met very nice people in Lille and sometimes I miss them.

On the 11th June 2011 it was my 50th year since graduation at the University of Florence, I invited my friends, Clients and of course I got a ticket and hotel for my Daughter and she was looking forward to see the ceremony and meet people that she had not known before.

Sadly a couple of day before she told me that she was not feeling well enough to travel. I was sorry but not too worried as she was in good health, working very hard.

The ceremony went very well and I was given a very nice gold medal to remember this important occasion. I was very happy and I was making sure that the University Catering had all tables with the correct names of the Guests, when I received a call from the London Hospital telling me that my Daughter had just died. You can imagine how I felt, but I could not let all my Guests down by going to my hotel to cry.

I found myself to be a good host as a lot of people had come from far away . I do not know how I managed, but I did and I did not start to cry until they left. I am crying now after ten years, remembering how I felt then.

My Daughter was not only running the office but even when she came to visit me in Lille I can still see her cleaning and cooking for me and I am still in great pain.

I had organized everything for her to have a good life and all had been for nothing.

Studying the Tax System in Malta I decided to go there, my Daughter have never been there, so I had no memories. A few months later I was flying from Heathrow Airport to Malta, and the plane was delayed by one Hour.

I asked the flight assistants if I could get a seat because of my age and very kindly they got me one.

A few minutes later a Maltese Lady came and told the flight assistants that she has high blood pressure and she also need a seat. The delay was long and of course we started talking. She had been to visit her two Sons in London, one an Opera Tenor and the other a Modern Dancer that was rehearsing Swan Lake. We exchanged business cards and went separate ways to our homes.

This Lady was very attractive with hazel eyes and I judged her to be a kind person, so I decided after a couple of days, to give her a call. I was not looking for a relationship, but to get to know people outside my work. Also she was much younger and I did not think she would be interested. She agreed to meet me at Castille and came with her convertible nice car. She drove me around to see nice places, explaining what they were and making the tour very enjoyable. At the time I was living in Valletta in a nice flat with a lovely view of the Port .It was time for dinner and she suggested a Restaurant close to my flat. At the end of the dinner I was fumbling with my pockets and she paid for the dinner. I thought that perhaps it was a Maltese custom so I felt obliged to offer her a drink at my flat. I think because of my age she felt safe and accepted.

When in ny flat I got tempted to try but she obviously said no. A few days later, thanks to one of her Friends that had met me, she accepted to see me, and to this day she is looking after me very well. We had quite a few good holidays together: Rome, Florence,Dubai, Cuba, sailing the Greek Islands, also P&O Cruise to Athens, Santorini etc. And more.

Rosalie has shown me many places in Malta and introduced me to very nice people, and I have been accepted by her Family and her Sons. Occasionally we go dancing . When my Italian Clients come to Malta, Rosalie THE LOVE OF MY LIFE, is always with me and helps to have interesting meetings and enjoyable lunches and dinners.

From May to September we are Members of the Sliema Pitch social Club that has deck chairs, umbrellas, open air swimming pool with sea water, bar and a good Restaurant. I try to swim everyday and enjoy it very much

During normal times I I am continuing my usual work with Italian Clients in U.K and Malta and thanks to internet one can work from home and contact different Countries . I have interesting projects in different Countries that I hope to realize even if now everything is very difficult.

Life in Malta is usually good, safe and good weather, helps to forget that it is such a small island. I am always surprised how many interesting buildings from old Civilisations are here and also many works of art. To this date I have not been able to see everything. There are also good theatres and active cultural life.

Usually but especially during this Corona virus Lockdown, Rosalie cooks and brings me excellent food that keeps me healthy .We do not know how long this problem will continue and what financial consequences will be, we can only hope for the best. But really we are all starting to worry about the future as it looks like there is no cure and the vaccine is a long way off, therefore we are not safe. As I am writing I am not allowed out of my flat because of my age, it is getting hard, thinking I could be swimming and going out with Rosalie.

Because of this,sad parts of my life start coming back to upset me.

As I am still stuck inside my flat I will continue with my memories My Second Wife, having lost me three houses in London, after the death of my Daughter, went to live in the Villa in Spain. I had donated this property to my Second Daughter when she was nine years old . Sadly she died on 11/06/2011 and at this point the property, because my Daughter was not married and had not children, 50% came to her Mother and 50% to me. My Second Wife was there for several years until her tragic death on 12/12/2017. She was living alone and had not much contact with the outside world, from what I understand.

One day in late November 2017 my next door neighbours noticed that there was not light in the Villa, and they know that my Wife went out to buy groceries, only once a week, so they called the Police. The Police came, went around the Villa, but could not see anything wrong, so they went away. A few days later my Step Son and his Spanish Lady Companion came, again they called the Police, but they could not see anything wrong. My Step Son went back to England thinking that, perhaps the Mother was there. Of course she was not, so he came back to the Villa, this time with the police and the Fire Brigade. The Authorities then broke into the Villa and did not let my Step Son in, because the Mother was in advanced state of decomposition and her death Certificate states 12/12/2017 as estimated date of death.

According to Spanish Law we had to pay Euro 4,000 to have her remains cremated, if payment was not made they would have left her there, and Euro 2,000 to have the place fumigated and cleared. My Step Son changed the keys and for about two years I did not hear from him. After this time I asked him for a copy of the keys as I might want to stay a few months in Spain or may be longer. At this point he said that I could not have the keys and stay there. I had treated him as my own Son and did not expect such reaction . I got my Solicitor to write to him but realized that he thought that the place was his and he was not giving me the keys.

A few months ago, his eldest Brother Constantine contacted me, after many years, he had been as a child in the Villa and I explained everything to him.

Because of my Step Son Valentine behaviour, I decided to seek legal advice and do everything according to Law.

My Wife had five children:
Constantine
Valentine
Ethelbert
Christopher
Ada Emilia

So the Mother 50% share goes as follows:
Constantine 10%
Valentine 10%
Ethelbert 10%
Ada Emilia 10%

As Ada Emilia died her 10% is divided as follows : 50% to me and 5% to the Brothers, hence each Brother has 11.25% and I have 55%.

So the Villa will be divided like this and Valentine will not have 100% but 11.25%.

This late in life I did not need this but I have always moved forward, so it will be this time.

Today 06/06/2020 the over 65 years old are allowed out!

Practically three months inside felt a very long time!

In Malta this Corona virus has been well managed, lets hope that when the borders are open, from first July, the infection will not come back.

I have decided to buy two books, one called Homo Sapiens and the other Homo Deus by the same Author Yuval Noah Harari. He is a Professor of History at Tel Aviv University, I have followedsome of his lectures and found them very interesting.

Once I read these two books I will probably buy his latest called " 21 Questions for the 21st Century".

I am trying to get a bit of intellectual stimulation and forget that the overall situation is not good.the solution will not come for a very long time and I must try to rise above it.

Today 06/06/2020 the over 65 years Old are allowed out!

Practically 3 months inside felt like a very long time.

In Malta this Corona Virus has been well managed, lets hope that, when the borders are open, from the 5th July 20, the infection will not come back.

Activities at present are very slow, all projects are on hold.

I decided to buy two books one called HOMO SAPIENS and the other HOMO DEUS by the same Author Yuval Noah Harari a Professor of History at Tel Aviv University.I have followed some of his lectures and found them very interesting.

Once I read these two books I will probably buy his latest called "21 QUESTIONS FOR THE 21ST CENTURY" I am trying to get a bit of intellectual stimulation and forget that the overall situation is not good.

The solution will not come for a very long time.

Printed in the United States
By Bookmasters